ISABELLA DUATE J.
Poems From My Soul
Words Too Hard To Say Volume I

POESIA PERENNIS EST

★. · ° Isabella Duarte Jimenez ° · .★

Poems From My Soul

Isabella Duarte Jimenez

★.·° *Isabella Duarte Jimenez* °·.★

© 2025 Isabella Duarte.
All rights reserved.

No part of this book may be reproduced, stored in a retrieval system, or transmitted in any form or by any means—electronic, mechanical, photocopying, recording, or otherwise—without the prior written permission of the author.

Certain quotes used in this book are from public domain sources, including "Poesia perennis est" (Poetry is eternal).

Words Too Hard To Say Volume I

Second Edition

ISBN: 979-8-218-63176-5

⁺°★° Poems From My Soul °°★°⁺

For anyone and everyone
who needs to read words
that makes them feel something.
For the young, for the old,
for the joyful, for the sorrowful.

Forever grateful towards
mom and dad
who always support me,
and to my fifth grade teacher
Ms. Slocum,
who got me into poetry
and now this book exists.
Thank you.

-*I.D.J.*

★. ·˚ Isabella Duarte Jimenez ˚· .★

Quick Note

These poems will get better the more you get into the book!
    The first poem in this book, *That Long Night*, was the poem that made me realize that I could write good poems easily. I wrote it when I was around ten or eleven, I was in fifth grade. That poem was the seed to this whole book.
    If you were wondering, the flower on the cover is a *Magnolia*. I chose it because one of the many things it represents is **perseverance**. I felt like Magnolia's representation of perseverance matched my first book, since it took me around three years to fully write it, and perseverance was very needed to make this dream reality.
    I hope you enjoy it.

Isabella Duarte Jimenez

That Long Night

Every day is cold
because it's winter
I try to sleep at night
but something changed my mind

The moon in the window
makes me take a minute
Stars shine bright
and with that light
I can't sleep at night
in the long, cold night

Today, Like That Night

In school
every day is cold
but today
it is not

Today is warm
with a chilly breeze,
and in the classroom
there's sunlight in the window

That light
it's like that night
with the bright light
of the moon through the window

Confidence

Confidence, confidence
is all I want
but diffidence, diffidence
is all I got

While walking through the hallways
I try to look up
but my confidence banishes
so downward I look

But when I see the other girls
full of confidence
not diffidence
they inspire me to be
positive
convinced
satisfied with myself
But that confidence is temporal
it vanishes in seconds

I lay in my bed
with my heart full of hope
that someday, sometime
I will be
confident, not diffident.

Were We Friends?

I thought we were friends
but that's where it all ends
I gave you my trust
and you broke it into pieces
now that is broken
it will never be golden

Now that I'm older
I know I have to be colder
because I don't want to believe
in something, someone
that will stab me in the back
and will leave
a big scar

Strangers

I never thought you would like me
and would let me in
We laughed and smiled together
but it didn't last forever
After that day, we became strangers

Not a little of eye contact
not a single word came across
I still feel close to you
but that was never true

Just strangers we are
and will always be
unless someone takes the first step
then, everything would change

How I Changed

I grew up
and I flew away
I left everyone and my memories
and headed for new journeys

As I grew older and mature
I realized I wasn't
who I was before
Yesterday became tomorrow
and today became the past

I met a lot of people
but few of them stayed
I was lied to, laughed at
and talked about
but I still kept my head up
even if it hurt deep inside

Nobody knew what I felt and thought
and even in the worst
I still fought
I turned myself away from people
not letting myself get hurt again

And I changed a lot
but I still felt miserable
and not enough

Buried Feeling

I felt a lot of pain
like if I was attached to a chain
While crying in the rain
my positive thoughts drained away

I tried to trick my brain
but it wouldn't go away
I was stuck in a memory
that was supposed to make me happy
yet I cried when I thought about it

The memory wouldn't go away
so I distracted myself
from those happy days
that made me cry

After a long time
I forgot about it
Continued my life
without showing the feeling
that was deep inside
forgotten
and buried

Drowned By My Feelings

I found comfort in silence
fell into the dark
and now that I'm in there
I can't see the light
Drowned by my feelings
here I am
hiding everything
deep inside

Here I am once again
my depressing thoughts flooding me
I thought I found a solution
but the frustration comes once again

People asked me if I'm fine
I gave them a fake smile
and said *yes, no need to worry*
but my sadness kept going

When they walked away
the smile faded
because I'm being drowned
by my feelings

Away

There goes the bell
and another day
faking a smile
forcing a laugh
saying that I'm alright

Lying to myself
the day goes away

⁺°★₀° *Poems From My Soul* °₀★°⁺

Birthday Girl

Mom wakes me up
singing happy birthday

but it is only a reminder
that I'm getting older

soon I'll be like my mom
then like my grandma

It is just a normal day

For once
I am the birthday girl

I'm The Girl Who

A silent cry
is the loudest scream
a single tear
holds the strongest pain

I saw my own eyes
in the reflection of my mirror
and they seemed different
after all I've been through
The things that I saw
changed how I see the world

I am not the girl
I was before
nor I think
how I used to
Now I am different
from who I used to be

I´m the girl
who dreams
but does not believe

I'm the girl
who is sad at night
and in the morning
is with a big smile

I´m the girl who cries quietly
and is screaming inside

Lost In Myself

When I went out to the world
it welcomed me at first
I met people
who I admired
so I tried to be like them

Throughout the years
the world changed me
and the people I knew
changed me too

Because of that
I don't know myself anymore
All the memories I had
of me being myself
seem like a past
that I never had

Now I'm a combination
of people I've met
people I've lost
and people I know

I don't really know
who I am
out of all the people
I once was

I am a stranger
when I look into my eyes
The windows of the soul
that is lost in a sea of worlds

★·˙° *Isabella Duarte Jimenez* °·˙★

I'm Someone
People think I'm someone
someone that I´m not

So I try to hide feelings

Just once more

Hiding

Here I am once again
nothing to see
nothing to hear
Even in the crowds
I'm lonely
Solitude to me
tastes like honey

Scared of people's judgy eyes
of cruel words
and disapproving sighs
So I hide myself
hoping it won't be forever

With the mask that I wear
people think I'm someone
With the way I behave
people think I am
who I show them that I am
however, it is all an act

Something keeps me
from being who I really am

Oh, Those Quotes

The quotes that reach my soul
and the darkest corners
of my fragile heart
are sad but true

How I wish I wrote like that
With a mind full of thoughts
and a broken heart full of hope
what would keep me
from writing beautiful words?

What am I supposed to do
when some simple words
shatter my soul?

The Right Friend

I always tried to find
the right friend for me

Someone who understands me
and cares about me

Self Talks

Nobody listened to me
so I listened instead
Nobody is interested
in what I have to say

Even if the words
were torturing my ears
I listened
never spoke
Even if the words flooded me
I didn't dare to talk

The fear of being disliked
kept me quiet
The fear of disappointment
made me silent

I thought through the night
about what I should've said
and I talked to myself
about all I couldn't say

Enough

Sometimes
I don't feel enough
even if I´m
already good

Some of my friends
think I´m perfect
tell me I´m perfect

But if they could see
the truth behind my smile
they would think
otherwise

Gone

There was something between us
but now there's nothing more
than distance

It's not like I cared
Maybe I do

It's just one lost friendship
without a broken soul

After some time
I realized
that life's like that
People come
and walk by
leaving me
and the memories behind

Moon

The moon is lovely
isn't it?

It's smiling at me
with it's yellow light
It's telling me
that it's safe to sleep

It will hold my tears
carry my worries
keep my darkest secrets
from far away distance

And I know it's 11:09 pm
the moon tells me
I should be sleeping
But it's yellow smile
is a beautiful reason
to stay awake all night

Oh moon, why are you so lonely?
Yellow and half smiling
beautifully mysterious

Oh moon, Why do you hide yourself?
I only want to admire your beauty and your grace
I wish I could be like you someday

Rocky Landscape

The sun is setting
once again
The sweet breeze playing
with my locks of hair

The rocky mountains
decorating the horizon
The stars appearing
to welcome the night
Dulcet melodies
dancing around my ear
and a small urge
to go to sleep

Words

I wish I wrote the way I feel
without mask
without filter
Deep and intense
painful, overwhelming

Ineffable feelings lead to
beautiful words

Words that might never be written
things that I never get out
because no one was willing to listen
or I wasn't willing to share

If I write how I think
how I feel
will people listen?
Or will I listen to myself?

Will I finally know
what I feel?
Or will I just ignore it
like I did all these years?

Off

I am not doing my best
I´m waiting for everyone
to do the rest
I´m wasting my time
I´m wasting my life

The pathetic distractions
hypnotize me
Leading me
to a different path

Turning my brain off
my life off
my purpose
off

We're Poets

We´re poets
darling
we don't say what we think
we write what we feel

We write because people won't listen
We write because we need to know
what we can turn feelings into
We write because words are better on paper
than they are in the air

We
poets
are the artists
because nobody wanted to turn us
into art

We
poets
want to someday be
the poem
not the poet

Knowledge

Knowledge changed her heart
and also her soul

Knowledge changed
her point of view
It changed
her whole world
Then, because of it
she trusted a few
and believe not a word
that others spoke

That knowledge consumed her
keeping her awake at night
Not letting her sleep
breathe
or dream

She wished to not know such things
so she would live in peace
However, she was grateful
that she knew
because then
nothing could harm her

She knew
that what you don't know
can't harm you
So if she knew everything
should she be afraid?

Alone and Lonely

Alone and lonely
are very different

Being alone is a decision
being with yourself
and no one else
Some people think it's sad
some people think
that it is a paradise

Being lonely is a feeling
of being left out
disconnected
different
Of being in others´ worlds
yet never being seen
never being heard

So the question is
am I alone
or do I just feel lonely?

I want to be

I want to be the rose
that you see in the garden
I want to be the butterfly
that flies freely through the sky

I want to be the flame
that burns and keeps you warm
I want to be the glass
that's shattered and sharp

I want to be the moon
that shines in the dark
I want to be that quote
that once is read
is never forgotten

I want to be the tune
that you wish you knew the name of
I want to be the drop of rain
that helps a flower grow

All of these are beautiful things
some dangerous
some ethereal
Some will hurt you
some will make you smile
Some are hard
but worth to find

Some are simple
but beautiful at the same time

Broken, Empty

Broken promises
broken trust
empty words
empty souls

Tears that hold
the weight of worlds
Nights spent
crying alone
Memories are clouds
that cover the beautiful sun

The empty wish of being with you
the broken hopes when I lost you
the big scar over my heart
that everyday reminds me
of you

Unsaid words

Why is it that
when I have so much to say
so much to feel
words don't come out?

Ineffable feelings
unsaid words
distant thoughts
forgotten dreams
all in one
single tear

Burning sky

The sky is burning
when the sun kisses the horizon
and the blue shades start
to fill the sky

The beautiful flame
burns the sun from a distance
and it burns the clouds too
making them a pink cotton candy
orange too

After a long day
the sky is burning
Just like a phoenix
the sun will rise again
shine brightly through the skies
and once more
say goodbye

Dying every night
to let the moon breathe
Dying every night
to let to moon dream

But of course
the sun never leaves
because the moon wouldn't shine
without the sun's gleam

Tired

Yes, I'm tired
I'm tired of the people
the routines
the excuses
the distractions
the lies
the goodbyes
the world

So yes, I am tired
very tired
Tired in every single way
However
I won't give up

Not when I'm
so close to my goal
my dream
Not when people
believe in me
support me
Not when I want to
make a difference
I need to

So yes, I am tired
but I won't stop

Tired
but I have goals

Mood Problems

Can't you understand
that my mood changes?
I can't control it
I can't stop it

From happy
to mad
From joyful
to sad
And it's not my fault
that it goes all around

The blue clear skies
turned to gray in one night
and the clouds adorned
the vivid blue color
Then the clouds changed
the mood of it all
just like my thoughts
affect my heart

I can't control
the mood problems that I have
Don't they understand
that it's out of my hands?

Eye Contact

Eye contact
tells things
that the mouth can't say
An unspoken language
no sound
no words

Eyes are the windows of the soul
it's odd but true
Eyes tell stories of their own
things they've seen
things they've lived

No other pair of eyes
has seen the things mine have
No other pair of eyes
tell stories the way mine do

The art of eye contact
it's a strange
but lovely thing

Mamá

Nueve meses en tu vientre
nueve meses de esperanza
nueve meses de paciencia
nueve meses de esperar

Aunque aún no me conocías
cada día me diste amor incondicional
Me diste lo mejor
Sonreíste sin dolor

Te quebraste la espalda
por un futuro mejor
Eres una guerrera
mi ángel guardián

Eres mi luz en la oscuridad
mi ancla en la tormenta
mi sombrilla en la lluvia
mi árbol en el sol

Y aunque no eres perfecta
todo lo haces con amor
Porque todo lo que quieres
es un futuro mejor

⋆. · ° Isabella Duarte Jimenez ° · .⋆

Mamá (English Version)

Nine months in your womb
nine months of hope
nine months of patience
nine months of sitting tight

Although you did not know me yet
you gave me love that was unconditional
You gave me the best
you smiled without pain

You broke your back
for better coming times
You are a warrior
my guardian angel

You are my light in the darkness
my anchor in the storm
my umbrella in the rain
my tree in the sun

And although you are not perfect
you do everything with love
Because everything you long for
is better times to come

Papá

Me enseñaste a pelear
me convertiste en una guerrera
No hiciste cosas por mí
para que aprendiera a hacerlas por mi cuenta

Encuentras humor en todo
y siempre quieres que aprenda cosas nuevas
Me llevas la corriente
aunque mamá piense que estás demente

Me enseñaste a analizar
y ahora soy independiente
Aunque no siempre estás de buen humor
me haces reír un montón

Criar a una hija no es fácil
pero lo haces sin temor

Papá (English Version)

You taught me to fight
you turned me into a warrior
You did not do things for me
so I could do them on my own

You find humor in everything
and always want me to learn new things
You follow my lead
even if mom thinks you´re weird

You taught me to analyze
and now I´m independent
Although you are not always in a good mood
you make me laugh a lot

Raising a daughter is not easy
but you do it without fear

Poems From My Soul

Time

Time
it slips out of my hands
Nothing can stop it
it keeps going and going
a never ending cycle

Time
precious as gold
People undervalue it
wasting it away

Time
the oldest thing around
It sees people be born
and say goodbye

Time
it's slipping out of my hands
and yours too
Not noticing right now
but in the future, we will think
That's what I should've done

⋆. · ° Isabella Duarte Jimenez ° · .⋆

This Is How It Is Now

The words that you said
the letter that you gave me
the promise that you broke
the trust shattered in two

Everything you said
I remember and always will
The words on repeat
going over, once again

The way I feel
when I think of your name
What I think
when I see you again
I guess we could pretend
that what happened was just a dream

It's not my problem anymore
it never was, to begin with
So go ahead
I won't make you stay
whatever you decide
I won't change your mind

Everything has changed
but it still feels the same

(This poem was inspired by the song Kaleidoscope by Chapell Roan)

Persistence

Standing up when you fall
even if no one
gives you a hand
Climbing the mountain
when everyone else
goes back
Studying at night
when everyone
is sound asleep
Working so hard
while the others
sit and watch

Nobody said it was easy
to be a flower growing
in the side of the road
But the persistent flowers
end up being the strongest ones

The bird that
didn't know how to fly
now travels
freely through the skies
And its happiness doesn't compare
to the pain it felt
while trying over again

Never Really Did

Went on picnics
slow dance at the beach
late night walks
midnight talks
Awkward eye contact
and rolling eyes
Holding hands
threatening with knives
Small fights
dancing under the stars

I did all this things
in my head
because that's what happens
when you're in a world
that's isn't yours

Fantasy it is
and always will be

I did all this things
but never really did

Dreamed with my eyes opened
different worlds
different stories
different lifes
different reasons

°★° *Poems From My Soul* *°★°*

I hid myself
I learned to fight
I stood up for myself
I solved puzzles
I lied and lied
I became a queen
a wanted girl
a thieve from the slums
a billionaire so young
a human in another world
a girl who hasn't decided
and the list goes on

I was all this things
but never really was

I've read too many fairy tales
lived these things through the pages
things that did not happen
and never will

Isabella Duarte Jimenez

But I got Used To It

Keeping my smile
is hard
but I got used to it
Being positive all the time
is hard
but I got used to it
Shattering inside
while faking a laugh
is hard
but I got used to it
Being happy for other people
even if I did not make it
is hard
but I got used to it
Moving on
pretending I forgot
is hard
but I got used to it

Feelings are a glass of water
they fill up the glass
You keep fake smiling
forcing laughs
and the glass keeps filling up
Head up
shoulders squared
more water added to the glass
Crying at night
smiling during the day
More and more water fills the glass

Until one day
the glass got full
and the tears slipped
without permission

The glass overflowed
so did my capability
of holding everything
deep inside

Thought about silly songs
bit my lip
blinked rapidly
looked up

But the tears
the stubborn tears
won't go away

But I will keep
my fake smile

I will keep
my head up

I will keep
saying I'm alright

I will keep
living my life

The Clouds

That night
the clouds were crying
they cried so hard
sobbed so loud

That night
the clouds reminded me
that I wasn´t
the only one crying
the only one sobbing

What the clouds were crying over
I do not know
But what I was crying over
was not the pain anymore
it was not the rejection
It never was

But I was crying
over myself

The clouds quieted down
so did I
writing this poem

But the clouds
were still full of water
just like I
was full of emotions

Poems From My Soul

That night
it rained so hard
that when my tears fell
the clouds went mad

The clouds cry too
they cried with me
I cried with them

We both cried
we both screamed
we both rained
ourselves to sleep

Summer Is Gone

From the beautiful sunsets
and the sunny days
To the stormy nights
and gray dawns

The sun's rays on my skin
the soft drops on the floor
Birds singing melodies
the constant sound of rain

How I used to hate those summer days
the heat making my skin sticky
the sun making my head dizzy
Now I'm here
wind blowing
rain falling
fog rising

Why do I miss
the memory of
those beautiful blue skies
and the soft warmth?

Not Real

I saw your smile
but it was not real
I heard your laugh
but it was not real

I felt my hair
get caught in the wind
but it was not real
I felt the rain drops
fall on my skin
but it was not real
I danced to the music
in a beautiful dress
but it was not real

Was it a dream?
Or just a nightmare?
Was it real?
Or just fantasy?
Why can't I tell apart
my ideas
from reality?

It is all making me crazy
things that happened
but never did

Living things
to wake up and realize
I did nothing

Million Pieces

They say
Follow your heart
But what if the heart
it's in a million pieces?
Which piece
do I follow?

The heart shattered
in little pieces of glass
was no longer
as strong as it once was

Someone told
the owner of the porcelain heart
to follow it
and happiness they would find
But little did that person know
that the heart was shattered
in more than two

Salt, Sugar

Salt
sugar
they both look the same
Little white crystals
in a bottle
or a cup

Salt
Sugar
no difference to the eye
Little rocks
just like sand

Salt
Sugar
so different in taste
one so sour
other too sweet

Salt
Sugar
just like
everyone
and the world

Salt
Sugar
which will you choose?
Will you trust your eyes?
Or will you read the label?

*. · ° *Isabella Duarte Jimenez* ° · .*

Salt
Sugar
don't trust it
before reading the label
or having a taste of it

Be careful with who you trust
you might think it's sugar
but you might end up adding salt
to your little life

Pawns

Everyone wants to be the queen
so powerful and capable
But no one is born
being strong or smart
you have you built yourself
just like the pawn

They think it's weak
the poor little pawn
They think it's useless
the most common piece
They don't value it
thinking that what it is now
it's more important
than what it can become

Pawns
the only piece
that deserves power
It's so weak at first
powerless
they say

It walks through the war
looking all around
admiring the queens
the rooks
the bishops
They all have power
they are all important

But do they deserve it?

Poor little pawn
can only go forwards
because it has nothing to lose

Poor little pawn
it keeps pushing on
surviving every move
not going back
And once it crosses the whole board
it gets what it deserves
it becomes a queen

It deserved it
that little pawn
It became a queen
it worked for it
survived all the way
But the other pieces
just overlooked it
They don't value
the hard work and discipline

Poor little pawn
so weak and powerless
at first
But poor little pawn
became the queen

We are all pawns
we are all being played
the thing is
what path will you choose?

Don't let the queens
rooks
bishops
knights
intimidate you

We are all pawns
future queens
but will you go
across the board
to get
what you deserve?

Crying Over Math

I couldn't see
the numbers through my tears
letters, symbols and numbers
flooded my head like a storm
fast and not making sense
The tears spilled
how could they not?

When frustration took over me
my silent cry began
I saw answers that I didn't know
how I was supposed to find

I tried so hard
and how stupid I felt
I couldn't keep up
Finding the x
in a sea of numbers
letters, symbols
is difficult
when you don't remember
how to sail

I've done this before
my brain told me
yes, I know I have
but I don't remember how
One never truly learns anything
we just remember it
until we forget

Broken, Not Fragile

Broken
not fragile

Nothing really broke me
and I was never fragile at all

Just a little scratch
and the walls shattered

I am broken
But was I ever fragile?
Was I not aware
I could break into pieces?

Rose, Petals, Thorns

I want to be that rose
that is beautiful and dangerous
delicate looking
but sharp as glass

With it´s pointy thorns
that are my words
it will keep every danger
at distance
so that the petals
that is my heart
will not break

But what I really am
and might always be
is the petal all alone
small and delicate

Just a single petal
not a full rose

Any Way

I see the world
and I'm ready to explore it
my heart says *let's go*
but my brain says *let's not*

Why am I so afraid
of getting hurt in any way?

Isabella Duarte Jimenez

Don't You Realize

Don't you realize
that the stars are falling
that the world is ending
that my heart is breaking?

Can't you see
the stars are missing
the flowers are dying
the mask is slipping?

Don't you notice
the lonely moon
the dried grass
the fake smile?

Why can't I
show how I feel?

The stars will comfort me
won´t judge me if I cry
Perhaps then
the moon will leave the sky

Leaving

Rain falling
skies cloudy
background noises
me all lonely

Standing there
in there middle of the rain
thoughts pass like thunders
all around my head

Possibilities
ideas
dreams
hopes
wishes

People pass by
will anyone say goodbye?
They just leave
without looking back

A Dream

It all feels
like a dream to me
not the unbelievable type
not the one that turns your reality
into heaven
But the type that
will never happen

A far away dream
a wish
a hope
a thought

Same Stuff

It's Monday, once again
same class, same life
The same faces
walking through the halls

I've tried my best
there's nothing else
for me to do
I have tried
and I have succeed
What is there left to say?

Summer

Blue clear skies
where once fog was
the sun shines bright
with its warm smile
Sweet gentle breeze
caressing my skin
it's time to relax
to laugh and smile

Birds sing
those happy melodies
Skin gets darker
hair gets lighter
We grow
we learn

One more summer
added to the list

Autumn

I watched the leaf fall
gracefully through the air
The wind tangled my hair
and it danced with the trees
There were clouds on the sky
everything is black and white

The leaf fell
all alone
softly and slowly
just like I do
More leaves fell
spinning through the air

The fog rises
taking my vision away
Trees change
to the autumn days
And I wonder why
time passes so fast
Can't I smile at the sun
one last time?

Backup

I was treated like a backup
a second option
last one chosen
the last one thought of

I was treated like the best
the most important
just when they
needed my help

But even though
I tried to be enough
I was still
the backup choice

Just a Wish

I can only wish
to not be here
but somewhere else

Perhaps I can only wish
to not be who I am
but who I want to become

Yet, it is only a wish
a hope
a dream
Perhaps it will soon
be my reality
or a wish
it shall remain

Because who am I
to wish and wait
for things to happen?

How Will I Know?

Who will answer
the questions I have?
Who will tell me
why I cry?

I indeed do not know
the answers
that might lay within myself
But perhaps
the answers are outside
But how will I know
if I´m stuck
being a child?

A prisoner of my mind
holded back by my feelings

How will I know
if I am stuck
in a small box?

Change

Here I am
in a world that isn't my own
I want to change it
but it has already changed me
So why not go out there
and be the change
I so much want to see?

For Myself

Don't do it for others
do it for yourself
because who will care about me
the way I care about myself?

Perhaps I´d like to know
who will be there for me
like I am there
for myself

But at the end
it's my life
my choice
my time
my future
my decision
it is mine
and mine only

So I shall be
the one
to make the choice

Queen

Where once a girl was
a woman there is now
If there is no crown for me to take
I will build my own from dirt
Even if the sun dies
I will not burn out

Because this princess won't give up
until she is queen
of her own kingdom

A girl she still is
but a woman
in her way of thinking
She looks small
but thinks big

Her mind
is her weapon

Isabella Duarte Jimenez

For a Reason

Everything happens
for a reason
The sun shines
the clouds form
The trees die
but flowers grow

Something beautiful
perhaps painful
something that
is not changeable

For Coach Katrina

Little Red Rose

Sweet and gentle
just like a rose's petals
Flowers here and there
blooming everywhere

Cold rainy days
walking all away
Letting the sun come
letting the rose grow

Pink and purple flowers
also will grow
all around
the little red rose

It felt strange
that little red rose
surrounded by
purple and pink flowers

But little red rose
did not mind that
because she knew
that in her own way
she was beautiful
as all the others

⋆.·˚ Isabella Duarte Jimenez ˚·.⋆

Time ticks by
without a warning
without a sign
It vanishes away
wondering if this
was all worth it

But if giving up is accepted
failing is also accepted
So yes, it was all worth the while
because spring will come
and everything will bloom

We are all roses
we truly are
how long
do you think we'll last?

For Coach Malia

A Painting Where Everything Changes

Painting a dream
in a beautiful spring day
where flowers bloom
where nature grows
where the fear of changing
no longer endures

Flowers will grow
lavenders, zinnias
sunflowers too
The clouds will cry
sending rain through the skies
The sun will come
smiling bright down at us

The seasons change
so do I
the flowers grow
so do I
Everything changes
everything grows bolder
everything gets older

Time
my old enemy
is waving goodbye
to these past memories

★· ·° Isabella Duarte Jimenez ° · ·★

A painting
where everything changes
Things flash before my eyes
birds fly across the skies

Everything can be beautiful
But what about my mind?
Can what's happening inside
affect the other's lives?

For Coach Payton

Small memories

Baby's breath
soft and small
just like snow
Little clouds
above your crown

The memories were fading
but came back once again
Smiling at little moments
I almost forget

Saying goodbye
is now a lot harder
How can something end
if it keeps beginning?

The summer days
came to an end
and with them
the green emerald shades

Autumn was welcomed
with little orange leaves
falling through the air
just like little pieces of fire

*. · ° *Isabella Duarte Jimenez* ° · .*

The clouds are rising
hiding the shining sun
The trees change
its colors to something new

But once autumn is gone
with it´s little auburn shades
red tulips say goodbye
to those cold but cozy days

Orange brown-ish trees
with gentle breeze
with a warm drink
it is all that I can think

I wish some simple things
stayed in my mind
but they are so tiny
that forgotten and buried
it's all they become
Once again
another memory is gone

⁺°★° Poems From My Soul °°★°⁺

For Coach Korae

Little storm

The skies are cloudy
it smells like rain
of the storms to come
Warning us about the days
that we will soon forget

The sky is gray
but I see colors in it
No birds around
only raindrop sounds
The dark day
cold weather
chilly breeze
and bad temper

The storm has passed
and with it
the colors finally shine
The flowers are stronger
the sun is brighter
the clouds are softer
and the smile is wider

Red roses grew everywhere
adorning the lonely grass
adding the soft color
to the simple life

Isabella Duarte Jimenez

Butterflies pass by
admiring the ethereal beauty
thinking *oh,*
the storm was worth it

The little light
was found at the end of the tunnel
and it was not a train in this case
it was the shining bright light
of the warming sun

Autumn has come
the leaves have changed their shades
and once again
the skies are gray
But this time
the happiness remains

They Will See

I tried my best
but they chose me last
I did everything I could
but they overlooked how hard I worked
I spent nights
crying over the spent time

I tried my best
and I got less
now I have to try
more and more and more
to be where I deserve

I tried to do more
but I got less instead
If I hadn't tried so hard
perhaps I'd have more

But that is the thing
they judge you on what you have
not how hard you've worked
to get there

Perhaps it's a challenge
maybe just to see
if I really care
But can't they see
my hard work
and dedication?

★ · · ° Isabella Duarte Jimenez ° · ·★

I know I messed up
messed up bad
but didn´t they think about
how hard I tried?

And just you see
I will come back for what is mine
and once I´m there
I will not leave

I tried once
I tried twice
I will try over and over
until I get what is mine

Don't see the glass
half full
see it half empty
Perhaps like that you´ll see
that you deserve more than you have
and you will dare to fill the glass up

They tried to shatter me
they did
just for one night
Then I got back up
ready to fight back

They will see
what I can do
what I can become

⁺°★₀° Poems From My Soul °₀★°⁺

Mark my words
if you try to break me
just know
that I am not fragile

Reality

The tears spilled
just once
that's all

After that
I got back up
accepted reality
and worked to change it

Because you see
if there is no kingdom to rule over
I will start my own

This is my reality
right here
right now

My dream?
that will be my reality
not right now
but pretty soon
it will be

I´ll change my reality
and theirs along with mine
I'll come by and take their spot
each time
going up high
until there's nowhere else to climb
because I will have reached the skies

Belongs

The stars are
in love with the moon
The clouds are
engaged to the sky
The sea kisses the sun
right at dusk

But still
in a world full of love
where everything belongs
it looks like I do not

Raindrops fell
for the rainbow
butterflies seek
the most beautiful flowers

It cannot be right
it just cannot be like that
In a world where
everything belongs
apparently, I do not

And I'm getting older
yet I never really had
someone to watch the stars with
and see the sun rise

(This poem was inspired by the song Falling Behind by Laufey)

Protect

Turn your words
into sharp blades
and I will protect myself
with my rock solid heart

Stab me in the back
while you hug me
yet I am wearing
an armor underneath
because I saw it all coming

A broken heart
can't love anymore
A broken heart
cuts deeply like a sword

A lonely soul
won't fear the world
A lonely soul
can do it all alone

Stronger

Where once love was
now there is fire in her eyes
Words that cut
deeper than any glass

Once there was compassion
now there is no mercy
That is what happened
when someone betrayed her

Running in the dark
daughter of the shadows
fast like thunder
mysterious as night

Eyes that are
like blades to the soul
in a world of secrets
where everyone is a betrayer
and everyone has been betrayed

That made her stronger
Yet is it possible
to get hurt again?

Autumn II

Everything is beautiful
yet everything is dying
The leaves fall
with the auburn shades
little pieces of fire
that are the leaves
through the air

The clouds are rising
hiding the shining sun
Fresh breezes say *hello
summer is long gone*

The scarfs and winter coats
that I once again wore
and that little smell
of the storms to come
warning us about the days
that we will soon call home

Be More

As sad as it may be
it's true as words can be
the thoughts revolve around my head
yet they somehow affect what I feel

The salty water is unleashed
drawing a cold stream down my cheek
yet no sound comes out

Work more
do more
be more
For yourself
for your future
for others

The flame helps you see
yet you don't notice that it is dying
that it's doing everything in its power
for you
just you

Eventually
the flame will burn out
giving its last breath
for you

Fantasies

Painting a dream
living a fantasy
reading realities
where everything's just wishes

Gets up with the sun
accompanies the moon
Talks to the stars
about delusional hopes

Sees life
unravel before her eyes
Things grow
and they die
but that
is the cycle of life

Dark skies
over my head
soft grass
beneath my feet

Angel eyes
looking into mine

My reflection
telling me I'm fine
that I will survive
that I will fight

⁺°★₀° Poems From My Soul °₀★°⁺

Because even by myself
I will prevail

She Was A Rose

She was a rose
in the hands of those
who kept the flower
just for its beauty
but threw it away
when it becomes
a withered rose

Took off its spines
so she was weak and helpless
Put her in a vase
a glass cage
where she could do nothing
just stand there and smile

The poor rose
so beautiful yet so small
isn't valued how she deserves
She is thrown away
when she is seared

We are all roses
we truly are
how long
do you think we'll last?

Discipline, Not Luck

I am so sick
of people calling me perfect
they say I'm lucky
I that became so good
from night to the morning

They think it's easy
that I have the talent
perhaps gifted
or more open minded

It is hard work
and nights of thoughts
It's hours of frustration
motivation and discipline

So no
it is not luck
I did not become like this
in one single day

It has been years
hours
weeks
months
that turned me
into what I am today

Perfect
they called me
Discipline
I said

You do realize
that I've come this far
because I've worked
so hard?

Opportunity

An opportunity I got
and I did everything to have it

But then
I saw it vanish

I tried to catch it
looking for anyway to have it
I cried countless night
thinking of what would've happened

I wish I got the chance
to go back in time
My expectations hurt me
thinking that I'd be happy

But I wasn't chosen
I wasn't heard
I wasn't the one
to get the place

What am I supposed to do
when every time I see them
having the opportunity
that was going to be mine?

Isabella Duarte Jimenez

Their smiling faces
and happy hearts
Of course I smile
and say I'm fine

And well…

that's how life is

I just kinda wish
It didn't hurt like this

Working

I have to work hard
I have to spend all those nights
working towards my goals

Everything that is good
it's not for free
How will I have the life I want
without working for it?

Maybe I am tired
maybe I need to rest
maybe I work too much
thinking my life is a test

Do not waste a second away
do not tell me to stop

I will dare
to claim the sky
and I will
defy the stars

I will dare
to dream big

Knowing the price
I have to pay
and willingly
working towards it

Perfect

Do not call me
perfect

For you don't see
how hard I´ve worked
how hard I´ve tried

How many days
I´ve spent
without a rest

I wasn't born like that
I created myself
and I am still doing so

For I will not rest
until I have success

My Poems

All these poems
are pieces of my soul
turned into words

These poems
are who I was
who I am
and who I might always be

There is no other way
to explain myself

What would be of the world
without poetry in it?

All my feelings
captured in words
The ink is my voice
in a world
where my actual voice
is a little noise

Isabella Duarte Jimenez

Love In Books

Where is real love?
Where did it all go?
Where is the love
I read about in books?

Where are the flowers?
The midnight walks?
Watching the sunrise
and dancing among the stars?

Do not tell me it is fantasy
for I shall not fall in love
if it is

Is it true
that it is all gone?
No more poems
under the moonlight?
No more sunsets
or beach dances?

If it is all fantasy
a fake idea
a hopeless dream
I shall not even try
to fall in love once

Brown Eyes

Eyes say more
than words can
When there's nothing left to say
the eyes keep telling stories

Just simple eye contact
unravels a sea of secrets
Just a little glance
unlocks rivers of feelings

My mind is a dark place
and with my pools of honey
they sweeten what is
the shadows of my mind

Eyes kissed by the sun
a hundreth sunsets in one place
where the sun neither rises nor dies
yet the stars still make company

A golden cloth
over autumn trees
Brown eyes
honey skies
simple smiles
messy mind
all combined

19th Century

Born in a century
where people are foolish
where they spend their time
on things that are stupid

I wonder how life would be
in the 19th century
Where long dresses were wore
and people danced in a ball
Where eloquent words were spoken
when manners were used

However
born in the 21st century I was

Where jeans are worn
and people play video games all night
Where words are as casual as they could be
where manners don't even exist
Where books are almost forgotten
and true art does not exist

If my soul and heart long to be
back in the 19th century
why was I born
over 200 years
after where I want to be?

More Than Words

Words on paper
is what everyone sees
Deep, complex feelings
is what I read

How could someone
notice that I know?
How could they
notice that I don't only
see the words
just like everyone does?

I feel the pain
the sadness
sorrow, happiness
that weighs down
on those simple
inked words

The Curse Of Being A Writer

I stare into space
and people ask
what are you thinking about?
How do I explain
the hurricane that is my mind?

The curse of being a writer
is that everything is in your head
the only way to share it
is to write it on paper
When spoken out loud
it sounds like nonsense

How do I explain
the weight of worlds
the memories of those
who have never lived?

The curse of being a writer
the stories in your head
the ineffable feelings
that are only understood when read

This is what I chose to be
and I hope I don't regret it
for people notice
that I see more than words
on paper

⁺°★° Poems From My Soul °°★°⁺

The curse of being a writer
feeling everything so deeply
complex thinking
and the old, everlasting
what if?

It might not be a curse
it is perhaps a blessing
It is both, I suppose
that there are million of galaxies
in the mind of yours

A Writer

Untold stories
our minds hold
Suppressed feelings
our hearts carry
Vanished hopes
our souls remember

Only people like me
can write them on paper
turn them into words
that touch one's soul

Is it just me
or is it normal to do that?
I do it so easily
that I don't realize
what I am creating

Is it talent?
I guess it could be
Is it my passion
or just another hobby?

I call myself a writer
yet a normal girl
people may see
The war that is my mind
is unnoticed
before the simple
human eye

Cried Over The Future

How many times
have I cried over my dreams
my goals, my wishes
my future?

How many times
has something so simple
remind me of
the thing that both
my heart and soul
long for?

Tell me, is it really what I want?
because I can't decide

I want to do everything
be everything

Yet there is no time
to be all at once

Who Am I To Be?

Daughter of a queen
daughter of a soldier

Raised to be strong
raised to be bolder

But now that I am older
I question if I'll be
the queen my mother was
or as strong as my father was

The real thing is
who am I to be
if there's everything to become
yet nothing to be?

The Mind Of A Poet

How funny
is the mind of a poet

How deep
their feelings are

How drowning
their thoughts are

How complex
their thinking is

How amazing
their eyes can be

How odd
is the mind of a poet

We see everything
yet we don't realize it

We feel everything
yet we suppress it

Then we wonder
why do such painful words
come out of our minds

The mind of a poet
is something in which you'll get lost in

Paper Under Ink

The tears I have cried
show how hard I've tried
yet still here I am
questioning my decisions

It doesn't seem right
to overthink about
what could've been
and what it is right now

Thoughts dance
around my head
keeping me awake
not letting me sleep

All this feelings are unleashed
when I turn them
into paper under ink

⁺°★₀° Poems From My Soul °₀★°⁺

Pretty Things

Pretty things take time
Just like pretty words
take time to think about
Just like pretty paintings
take time to create

Just like pretty flowers
take time to bloom
and pretty souls
take time to grow

Pretty things can be fast
as well
just as lightning
fast speed, beautiful light
Just as laughter
in one second
a heartwarming sound

Just as shooting stars
fast going, ethereal asteroids
Just as thoughts
a million per second

Everything can be pretty,
beautiful, breathtaking
you just have to finds its beauty

Don´t change the thing
but change your perspective

What I Don't have

Don't ask me to give
of what I don't have

So don't ask me to give love
for I barely have some
for myself

Don't ask me to give advise
because I don't think
my words will help

Don't ask me to help you
I can't even help myself

Yet I fake it day and night
smiling with my head up

Don't you realize
that I can't give
of what I don't have?

Just A Fantasy

I'm miles away
form the dreams I wish came true
and I'm holding on
even though I know they won't
I go back and forth between things
I don't know what to chose

I am lost in a big, wide world

This universe is like a fantasy
I'm living dreams to wake up
and realize they're not real
just a fantasy
made up in my mind

And I try, I try
but the outcome is just
not good enough

Another dream
that didn't
come true

Creating Myself

I am creating myself
my future
my beliefs
and values

Reading books
spacing up my mind
changing the way I think
the way I walk

Learning psychology
learning hacks
learning anything
that will help me grow

However,
it feels as if I am doing nothing
even if I am doing
way more than enough

Working on my current self
for my future self

Improving myself
because it is time to change
who I am right now
to who I want to be

Tired II

Oh, how tired I am
physically
mentally
emotionally

I know I have to work
to study
but I just can't help it
I feel drained, powerless

No motivation
I am only relying on discipline
Wake up every morning
with my tired eyes
my tired mind

Tell me
will it all be worth it one day?
Will I look back
at right now
and thank myself?

Perhaps I do not need a rest
but I need peace
I need my space
to work on myself

I will make these early mornings
and these late nights
worth the while

Type, Type, Type

Words, words, words
being rapidly typed
by my freezing hands

Feeling, feelings, feelings
being recorded
by these simple poems
I make sometimes

Thoughts, thoughts, thoughts
being exposed
by this book
I am creating

Work, work, work
to publish my words
my feelings
my thoughts
a piece of my soul

Poetry, poetry, poetry
comes out out me
just like a river
Easy words
rhythms, rhymes

Type, type, type
Pouring my heart out
Hoping you enjoy
this little corner of mine

Hard Work

Straight As
goals in mind
working hard
studying through the night

I know exactly what I want
I know who I want to be
I know what I have to do
to be where I want to go

I know I might come off as cold
as if I need no friends
only knowledge is what I need

My brain choses education
over friendships
I chose to work
over having fun

Because, you see
nothing comes for free

I am made to succeed
If I fail
I fear I might
fall apart

Straight As
Good reputation
yet, it doesn't feel enough

★·° *Isabella Duarte Jimenez* °·★

I am hard on myself
because good things
never come easily

My friends joke around
saying I should already be
in college

Don´t you see
that while I can
I will study, work
get as many knowledge
and education as I can?

And when I grow up
all these early mornings
and late nights
will pay off

I am doing it
for my future self

Though, sometimes
people´s words don´t
acknowledge
my hard work
and determination

⁺°★₀° *Poems From My Soul* °₀★°⁺

Their careless comments
shattered my walls
Their words
were stuck
in my mind

Telling me
that I should be better
Others telling me
that I am enough

But which voice
do I listen to?
Which voice
do I follow?

(Part of this poem was inspired by the song Are You Satisfied? by Marina.)

Best Friend

Always friends
not best friends
Not close enough
not trustworthy enough
not enough

Tried to fit in
and I got friends
However, not best friends

Some called themselves
best friends of mine
From time to time
I would agree
then I came to realize
that it was all a lie

I won't trust anyone enough
to call them
my closest friend
my best friend

We live in a word of liars
yet we trust people too much
We misplace our trust
we misplace our time
Then we ask ourselves
why it hurts like that

Liars

A world of liars
the world we live in
Lying from time to time
hearing lies
from others' mouths

In a world
where dishonesty
is common
how do we know
what is true and pure?

We know
that people lie to our faces
yet we believe
those sugar coated words
We fall in the trap
We are so foolish
to put trust in the hands
of a thieve
of a betrayer
a murderer
a *liar*

We say we hate liars
yet we lie ourselves
every
single
day

Settling For Less

Wishing for more
settling for less
then we ask ourselves
*why don't I have
what I deserve?*

Being able
to stand up for ourselves
We sit there in silence
keeping our thoughts
to ourselves

Yet we dare to wish
to dream and to hope
and do nothing about it
Just stay where we are
with what we have
and not try
to have our dream life

Afraid of failure
settling for less
knowing that
we deserve more
than what can be offered

Don't you want it bad enough
to stand up and face the fight?

⁺°★₀° Poems From My Soul °₀★°⁺

In this world
people are foolish
because they settle for less
when they could've had more

Isabella Duarte Jimenez

One By One

I will now let
my success be the noise
for I tried
and miserably failed

Now it is time
to start a new game
I will stay quiet
One by one
I will defeat
slowly but steady
I will rise up
where no one else
can get me

Because if I cannot defeat
all of them at once
I will defeat them
one by one

They stood there
watched me fall
not expecting
that I will rise up

One by one
will lose against me
I´ll try once
I´ll try twice
I´ll try infinite times

Mark my words
I'll win the game
prove myself
and smile at my success

Years Ago

The sky is now
as cloudy as my mind
The wind picks up
dust from the streets
The trees are now leafless
the pieces of fire
flying away

Tucked in bed
hot tea
to warm my heart
Rain sounds outside
cloudy skies over us

Thinking of those days
of the precious memories
when I danced in the rain
when the wind played
with my hair
All those years ago
when I was nine years old
Jumping over puddles
splashing everywhere

Thinking back
to those dark but
happy days
It was long ago
in a place
I used to call home

The Stars

The stars
as small as they may seem
are powerful

Their light shines
like little pears
decorating the dark cloth
that falls upon us

The small stars
accompany the moon
when the sun
left her all alone

All the stories
told by the stars
All the lights
across the sky

The night's freckles
the little diamonds
all above us

In the moonless skies
the stars are the only thing
that I can see
in this vast universe

Promise

The promise that
I made myself
to choose happiness
to live happily

To walk away
when there is something
I don't like
To walk away
when it's something
I don't want

Choosing myself
choosing my happiness
Choosing the life
that I
promised myself

Not forcing myself to be happy
but choosing something
that makes me happy

Not Until

I can't risk falling
of my throne
I can't let people
steal my crown
The crown that I
have built from ashes

I have my reputation
I am well known
I cannot risk
falling from the top

After all I've been through
to be where I am
knowing I still have
a road ahead to go
I can't let
my guard down

I can't rest now
not until I get what I want
Not until I am
who I want to be
Not until I have
the life I want

Close, Yet So Far

I am so close
yet so far
to my dream
my goal

I can see it
just around the corner
it's just that
my legs won't let me walk

I am so close
yet I am stuck in this place
Something is holding me back
I just don't know what it is

It is a trap
a cage
Two chains
holding me back
from something that
is so close
yet so far

I see it vanish before me
something I worked for
something I wished for
something I deserved

It was all gone
in a blink of an eye

I'm Afraid

I'm afraid
all my hard work
all my late nights
will vanish before me

I'm afraid
that being so close
to my dream
it could just
not exist anymore

I'm afraid
that all my hopes
could break my heart

I'm afraid
that my expectations
will hurt me once again
just like they did
many times before

I'm afraid
of failure

A fear
that I cannot overcome
A fear
that chases me
day and night

Growing Up

I am growing fast
So fast that
I don't realize

My innocence
is slipping away
The fear of the dark
is now in the past

Now, a teenager I am
yet my childhood days
feel like yesterday

The loud laughs
and real smiles
All the things
I wanted to become
All the places
where I wanted to go

Even if I grew up
technically alone
I found comfort
where now I find none

How did
my young and foolish self
be so happy
even if she was all by herself?

⁺°★° Poems From My Soul °°★°⁺

I am growing fast
So fast that
I don't realize

So fast
that it scares me
to think about tomorrow
To think of
what it will be of me
To think of my future self

I remember my plushies
the stories before bed
the way I acted
the way I danced
All the shows
I put up for my mom
All those jokes
I did with my dad

I faced the world
and it changed me
Now I am
someone that I wasn't
I see things differently
with the same eyes

All those days
trying to fit in
All those years
my child-self
slipping away

Nothing To Give

All the city's lights
all the people lie
Thinking of who I am
waiting to watch me fall

They only come to me
when I have something
 I can give

And with nothing in hands
they leave to find
someone else
who can give them
all they want

I used to be a backup
somehow, I still am

Won't anyone stay with me
even if
I have nothing to give?

Just Me

In a time where I lost
all friendships
I found a friendship
one of a kind

I found out
that I could be
my own friend
Just like that
the world seemed
to fade away

I lost all my friendships
all at once
then I got used to
having my own company

Comforted by silence
not a soul around
just me and myself
the day flew away

The Past

The time that flew away
the time gone and lost
the time that I never before
thought I´d ever long

Thinking of memories
I will soon forget
Thinking back
to those lonely days

All the time
is flying away
vanishing without warning
fading without notice

The few pictures I have
are piled away
in a corner
where the memories
are with them
Put away
and forgotten

Now I focus on the present
the one that feels true and real
Even though
the memories I forgot
the past seems to become
what I live right now

⁺°★°° Poems From My Soul °°★°⁺

It seems that
I am living the past
that I tried to forget

It seems that I
am living it
all over
once again

Overflowed

The tears were spilled
my feelings overflowed
Multiple voices in my head
not one clear
for me to understand

I just can't figure out why
I became the way I am
I don't understand
where all these tangled feelings
came from

My words don't come out
as I'd like them to
they get stuck in my head
caught in a cage

My heart will soon explode
because of the seas it holds

My mind
occupied by thoughts

My mouth
with not a single word

Helped Myself

It seems like I somehow
healed my own wounds
as if I was
my own therapist

It seems like I somehow
helped myself
not knowing how
I did it

I lifted myself up
I pushed myself forward
I held my own hand
in the storm that was my mind

I was there for me
when no one else was

I wiped my own tears
carried my own weights

Protected myself
from my own fears
and made myself
who I am today

My Old Self

All the memories
I will soon delete
All those times
I so much want
to forget

My old self
who constantly
reminds me of
someone who I am not
and might never be again

Can't Forget

Lost in memories
moments I can't forget
Unforgettable feelings
moments that are
fresh in my mind
even if a million years
have passed

It seems that
I can't let go
of something that happened
so long ago

Fragments of dreams
hopes in my heart
Silly wishes
I had at night

The lights went off
the flame burnt out
The blue skies became
gray once again

Reality woke me up
bringing me back to this life
making sure that I'd forget
those joyful memories

Isabella Duarte Jimenez

Future's Gonna Be

Future's gonna be okay
I keep telling myself
over and over
through the lonely days

Late at night
questions linger in my mind
thinking of what it will be
wondering what I'll become

Thinking of things
that were not so long ago

Imagining the future
that is not close enough
Dreaming of the future
I might soon live
Crying over things
that might happen to me

Once I told my mother
in the middle of the night
I am afraid
of what my future will be

Then I slept
the night away

Once again
I am thinking
the same thing

Only this time
curiosity
fills my heart
when thinking of the future
begins my mind

Future's gonna be okay
Future's gonna be okay
Future's gonna be okay
Future's gonna be okay
Future's gonna be okay
Future's gonna be okay
Future's gonna be okay
Future's gonna be okay
Future's gonna be okay
Future's gonna be okay
Future's gonna be okay
Future's gonna be okay
Future's gonna be okay

Future's gonna be
what it has to be
I am here
just to built
the life
I deserve

Isabella Duarte Jimenez

Acknowledgements

A million thanks to God, who gives me the wisdom and creativity to write these simple words and put them together to create poems, and who has blessed me and my family.

Forever grateful towards mom and dad, who always support me and help me, who raised me to be who I am today.

Thanks to my church community, who are always like a second family to me and bring happiness to my life every Sunday.

Thanks to my fifth grade teacher, Ms. Slocum, who taught me how to write poetry, and who made my last year of elementary school special.

Thanks to my friends who have supported me, made me laugh, and been with me when I needed them.

Thanks to you for reading this book and spending your time on this little piece of art I have made!

Sincerely,

-*Isabella Duarte Jimenez* ♡

Author's Note

These poems are a part of me, these poems were me, are me, and are part of me that will still exist in the future. These poems have seen me grow, not only as a person, but as a writer as well.

In this book, you read poems I have written from experiences, thoughts, feelings, wishes, hopes, dreams, and things that just felt right to capture in words.

If you relate to any poem I have written, or if just my words make you feel *something*, not just "oh, that is just another poem," then I shall be happy.

I started writing these poems for myself, but when I started to have a big pile of papers and the poems were really good, I decided to write them for whoever is willing to read them and acknowledge my hard work.

I have to mention that these are poems that I have written from fifth grade to seventh grade, so you can see my writing growth. These poems have grown with me, and now I have the opportunity to put them out in the world.

I hope you enjoyed my feelings, thoughts, hopes, dreams, and wishes captured on paper, enjoy this little piece of my soul turned into words.

★. · ° *Isabella Duarte Jimenez* ° · ★

Award Recognition

Winner of Personal and Confessional Poetry Category

Poems From My Soul was honored with the *International Impact Book Awards* in July of 2025.

With deepest gratitude to the judges and to every reader who found a reflection of themselves in these pages.

About the Author

Isabella Duarte Jimenez is the author of several poetry collections that reflect a thoughtful and honest voice. Born in Colombia and raised in the United States from the age of ten, she writes in both English and Spanish, drawing deeply from her heritage and personal journey. Isabella began writing poetry at eleven, and her earliest stories, which were penned in childhood, became the seeds of her literary path.

You can find her Instagram: @isaduj21

www.ingramcontent.com/pod-product-compliance
Lightning Source LLC
Chambersburg PA
CBHW031645040426
42453CB00006B/213